Please return/renew this item by the last date shown

worcestershire
countycouncil
Libraries & Learning

CONTENTS

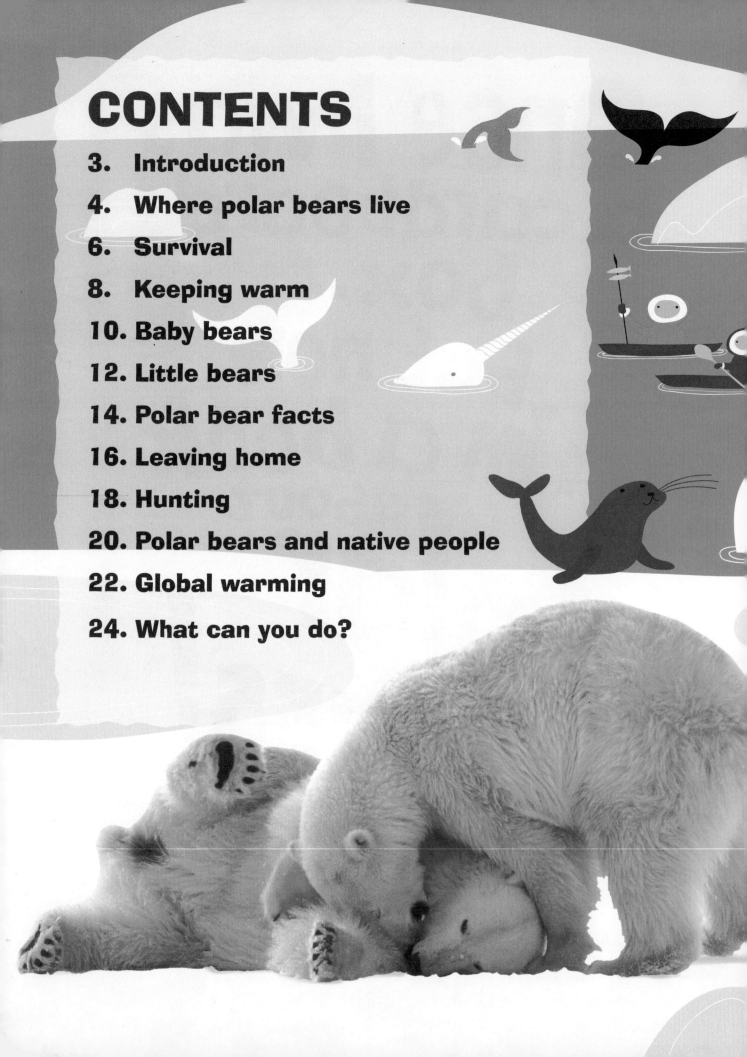

ONCE I WAS A CARDBOARD BOX... BUT NOW I'M A BOOK ABOUT POLAR BEARS!

I started my life as a cardboard box, but now I've been turned into a book!

Books are usually made from three things:

PAPER for books is usually made from wood. Old comics, newspapers, magazines and other card and paper are turned into new paper. This is called recycled paper. It is often more expensive than brand new paper, but it saves trees from being cut down and saves energy.

BOARD is used to make the stiff cover of a book. It is often made from recycled paper and cardboard and is called greyboard.

PLASTIC: the shiny cover of most books is made from very thin plastic called laminate. It is a bit like cling film.

This book is made only of recycled paper and board. We didn't use any plastic on the cover, which is why it isn't shiny.

So, what is this book about?

POLAR BEARS (and a bit about boxes!) The polar bear is in danger of extinction. This book tells you all about polar bears and how they can be helped to survive. The more we can help to care for our environment, the more chance the polar bear and other endangered animals have of surviving.

Where polar bears live

Polar bears live near the North Pole. Only five countries in the world have polar bears. They are:

- **Russia**
- **Greenland**
- **America, but only in Alaska**
- **Canada**
- **Norway**

Hello,
I live near the
North Pole.

CANADA

ALASKA

Polar bears never live in the same place as penguins, except in zoos!

GREENLAND

RUSSIA

NORWAY

Hello. I'm a cardboard box.

I was made in a factory in China from recycled paper.

Hello, I live near the South Pole.

Survival

Polar bears belong to the same family as other bears, but they are specially adapted for living on the Arctic ice.

FRONT PAWS like paddles for swimming. They have **SMALL BUMPS** called papillae to stop their feet slipping on the ice

LITTLE EARS so the bears don't lose much heat

GOOD SENSE OF SMELL to sniff out prey. Polar bears can smell a seal up to a mile away!

LONG NECK compared to other bears, to keep head above water when swimming

BIG PAWS for walking on snow and thin ice, and **STRONG CLAWS** for catching seals

BEAR FACT

Polar bears are the biggest predators on land, almost twice as big as lions and tigers.

The factory that made me sold me to another factory that makes toys.

100 little boxes of toy tractors were packed inside me.

BACK PAWS like rudders to steer

SHORT TAIL to help prevent heat loss

Keeping warm

It's difficult to imagine how cold it is at the North Pole. In winter, temperatures can drop to -45°C (-50°F), which is twice as cold as the freezers in supermarkets.

I was put
in a big container
with lots of
other boxes and
sent by sea
to England.

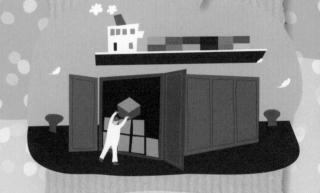

Luckily, polar bears have two layers of fur to keep them warm. Did you know that polar bears aren't actually white? Their fur is a yellowish colour, but it looks white because the hair reflects the light from the bright snow.

Each hair is a hollow tube like a drinking straw. This helps the bears dry off quickly after they've been swimming.

Then I
was sent to a
toyshop.

Baby bears

Polar bears usually have two babies each year. When the mother is pregnant she digs a den, called a maternity den, in the snow to keep the babies safe and warm.

BEAR FACT

The female bear has to gain at least 200kg when she is pregnant – that's the weight of 50 cats!

The cubs are born in November or December. A newborn polar bear is about the size of a loaf of bread. The cubs have no teeth. They are blind and have short fur.

The mummy bear stays with her babies in the maternity den until March or April. She does not eat, drink or poo during the whole time she is in the den. Imagine that!

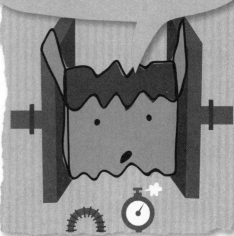

Little bears

Baby polar bears live in the den for the first few weeks of their lives. Their mummy keeps them warm. She feeds them milk that smells of seals or fish and they grow very quickly.

BEAR FACT
Polar bears sleep for 7-8 hours at a time, like humans. They also enjoy taking naps!

I was put in a big container and spent weeks there with lots of other squashed boxes.

After about four months the babies are big enough to leave the den. They play outside but they return to their mummy for milk.

A big truck came and took us to a recycling factory.

13

Polar bear facts

You will have found out lots of interesting things about polar bears by now, but here are some more facts for you to get your paws on...

- polar bears have 42 teeth

- they can gallop as fast as a horse over short distances, but they are so well-padded that they overheat

- when the ice is very thin, they crawl on their tummies so it doesn't crack

- scientists can work out the age of a polar bear by examining a slice of tooth and counting the layers – just like trees!

- each paw measures up to 31cm across, which is bigger than a dinner plate

- polar bears keep themselves very clean

- polar bears change colour slightly depending on the season or where they live

Leaving home

The baby bears get stronger and they learn how to do things that will help them survive as adults.

Their mummies teach them everything they need to know about living in the Arctic.

When the bears are about two years old, they are old enough to leave their mummies and start to hunt on their own.

The little pieces got mixed with water and we were made into a squishy mess called pulp.

The pulp went into another machine and we got made into brown paper.

BEAR FACT

Polar bears are happy to share their prey as long as they have enough to survive.

Hunting

Polar bears travel to the ocean to catch food. The bears can swim a long way. They have been found as far as 100km (60 miles) from land! That's about 4,000 lengths of a normal swimming pool.

Polar bears like to eat seals most of all. They hunt by sitting beside a seal's breathing hole in the ice. When the seal pops up to get air, the bear pounces and grabs the seal with its huge claws or teeth.

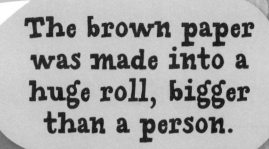

The brown paper was made into a huge roll, bigger than a person.

I think I was somewhere in the middle!

BEAR FACT
A polar bear's stomach can hold about 15–20% of its body weight.

Polar bears and native people

In the past, polar bears were hunted by the native people. The meat would be used for food and the fur was used for clothing. Nothing would be wasted as food was very hard to find near the North Pole.

Even though the native people hunted polar bears, they also worshipped them. Historians have found cave paintings of polar bears that are over 1,500 years old!

The native people may have learnt some important survival lessons from the polar bear.
Some people now think that the igloo was an imitation of the polar bear's maternity den!

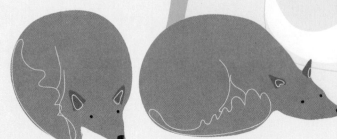

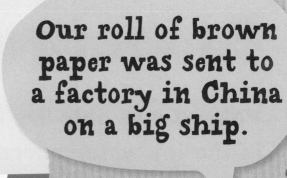

Our roll of brown paper was sent to a factory in China on a big ship.

The roll was put in a huge machine and we were cut into big sheets.

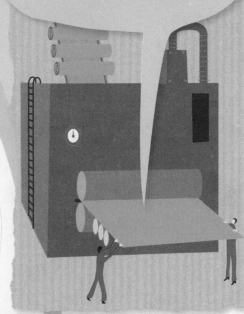

21

Global warming

Polar bears only live in very cold places – on ice and in the icy water surrounding it. Sadly, the Earth is getting warmer because of pollution. This is called 'global warming'.

As the earth gets warmer, the ice in the coldest parts of the world is slowly melting. This means that the polar bears' home is getting smaller and they have fewer places to hunt for food.

BEAR FACT
In 2008, the polar bear was officially declared an endangered species.

Some scientists think that if the ice continues to melt, many of the world's polar bears will disappear. Other scientists think that the polar bears will adapt by finding food in different places. They might start to eat salmon, like grizzly bears do.

The recycled paper was sent to a printing factory that makes books.

I was made into a book about polar bears!

Polar bears and native people

In the past, polar bears were hunted by the native people. The meat would be used for food and the fur was used for clothing. Nothing would be wasted as food was very hard to find near the North Pole.

Even though the native people hunted the polar bear, they also worshipped them. Historians have found cave paintings of polar bears that are over 1,800 years old!

The native people may have learnt some important survival lessons from the polar bear. Some people now think that the igloo was an imitation of the polar bear's maternity den!

Our roll of brown paper was sent to a factory in China on a big ship.

The roll was put in a huge machine and we were cut into big sheets.

What might happen to me next?

What can YOU do?

Recycling means making old products into new products. This uses much less energy than making things all over again, and helps to protect the environment. When rubbish is thrown away, it gets buried in the ground at something called a landfill site. This is bad for the environment!

- Recycle as much rubbish as you can at home – the easiest things to recycle are newspapers, plastic, cans and glass.

- If you have a garden, you can make a lot of food waste into compost.

RECYCLING ISN'T JUST ABOUT RUBBISH!

- Why not swap books, toys and games with friends when you have finished with them? Don't forget to ask your parents first!

- Take a shopping bag with you instead of using new carrier bags.

Making small changes can make big differences. Saving energy reduces greenhouse gas emissions which helps slow down climate change.

Try to do as much recycling as you can. You will be helping to conserve the world's resources and protecting natural habitats for the future.

WRITTEN by Anton Poitier
ILLUSTRATED by Melvyn Evans
DESIGNED by Clare Barber
EDITED by Georgia Barrington

PHOTO CREDITS
Front Cover © NHPA/photoshot · p.2 © Eric Baccega/naturepl.com
p.4 © iStockphoto · p.5 © iStockphoto · p.6/7 © NHPA/photoshot
p.8 © NHPA/photoshot · p.12/13 © Wayne R. Bilenduke (The Image Bank)/
Getty Images · p.14/15 © Terry Andrewartha/naturepl.com
p.16 © SeaPics.com · p.18/19 © SeaPics.com · p.21 © Eric Baccega/
naturepl.com · p.22/23 © Kennan Ward/CORBIS · Back cover ©
T. Davis/W. Bilenduke (Stone)/Getty Images

© 2009 Tony Potter Publishing Ltd, RH17 5PA
www.tonypotter.com

First published in the United Kingdom by Potter Books, an imprint
of Tony Potter Publishing Ltd

Printed in PRC